IMAGES
of England

WHITMORE REANS

Leicester Square, *c.* 1905. The square was the heart of the region with a fine selection of shops. Such was the popularity of the district that varied selections of postcards exist commemorating events and street scenes.

Lansdowne Road looking towards New Hampton Road East, 1925.

IMAGES
of England

WHITMORE REANS

Compiled by
Anthony Rose

TEMPUS

First published 2000
Copyright © Anthony Rose, 2000

Tempus Publishing Limited
The Mill, Brimscombe Port,
Stroud, Gloucestershire, GL5 2QG

ISBN 0 7524 2087 9

Typesetting and origination by
Tempus Publishing Limited
Printed in Great Britain by
Midway Clark Printing, Wiltshire

Dedicated to
Julie, Gillian and Anthony

New Hampton Road East, 25 August 1911. Soldiers of the West Riding regiment who were ordered to leave Wolverhampton for Salisbury Plain march out from Dunkley Street with 'full pack'.

Contents

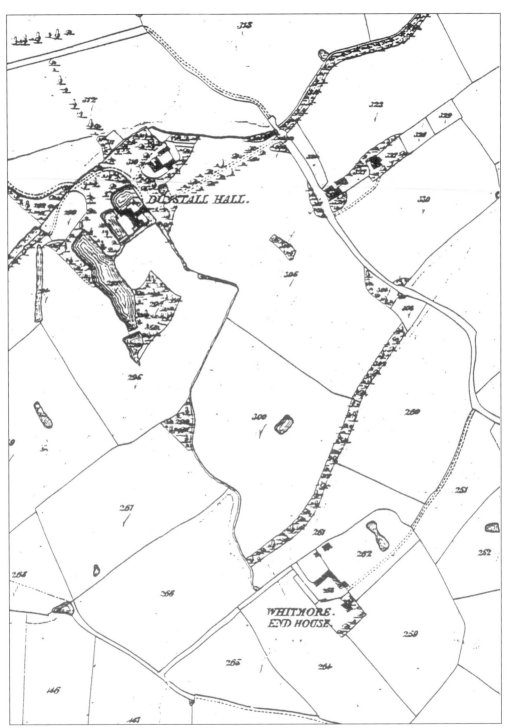

At the time of the 1842 Tithe Map the only notable building in the area we now know as Whitmore Reans, was that of Whitmore End House. Two roads ran through the area, Dunstall Lane, Staveley Road as we know it today, which ran from North Street in the town and pasted close to Dunstall Hall, and Whitmore End Lane, which later became known as New Hampton Road.

Introduction

There have been numerous theories put forward as to the derivation of Whitmore Reans. The most popular of these is that the original form of the name was *White-moor-reans*, this being due to the swampy nature of the area producing white fogs or mists which were frequently seen. The word *reans* denotes a furrow or gutter running parallel to ploughed land, these reans would have been used to drain the swampy ground. Natural transition would quickly have passed from *White-moor-reans* to Whitmore Reans.

Another theory is that the area was known as *Whitmore Ends*. It is a fact that before being named New Hampton Road the original cart track was called Whitmore End Lane. The theory is that following a number of transitions *Whitmore Ends* would have become *Whitmore-eans* and finally Whitmore Reans. However, the appendix to Shaw's Staffordshire Vol. 1, casts doubt on whether the area was ever known as *Whitmore Ends*.

At the time of the 1842 Tithe map the area was empty except for the buildings of Whitmore End House. Until 1850 there were less than fifty houses in the area, but that year Councillor Samuel Griffiths, an ironmaster who had somewhat of a shady reputation, built Whitmore Reans Hall on the site of the principal buildings belonging to Whitmore End House and Farm. The following year the Freehold Land Society purchased the remaining land and cut it up into streets and small plots and allotted the plots amongst its shareholders at a weekly subscription of 1s 7d. The society secretary was John Riches who is preserved in memory by Riches Street. During those middle years of the nineteenth century the population of Wolverhampton increased by almost 1,000 people per year, making a population in 1831 of 25,000 into 50,000 by 1851. Such was the increase that the town map of 1851 designated an area to be the site of a much needed new town. This satellite town was to be known as New Hampton though the name never caught on and the area continued to be called Whitmore Reans. The only traces of the attempts to change the name survive in the form of New Hampton Road.

Over the ensuing thirty years development spread out from around Whitmore Hall stretching down to Broad Meadows which was the site of the town's racecourse. The area had previously been known as Hungry Leas, a marshland area leased from Lord Darlington, later Duke of Cleveland, where at one time the town's sewerage had been discharged. The first meeting was held in August 1825 and racing continued there until the lease ran out in 1878.

The Corporation had for many years aspirations of purchasing the land for a public park and had held talks with the Duke of Cleveland in the 1860s but all to no avail. With the lease for racing due to expire, Alderman Samuel Dickinson made a new approach to the Duke with the intention of obtaining the land for the town. Although the Duke was not willing to sell the land outright, he did agree to make 50 acres available for 63 years at a cost of £300 a year for the first 42 years, and then £350 for the remaining 21 years, coupled with the option of purchasing the land for £20,000 at the end of the lease. The park was opened to the public on Whit Monday, 29 May 1882 and the option to purchase was taken up by the council in 1940 bringing the West Park into public ownership.

By the early part of the twentieth century Whitmore Reans had developed into a thriving community with a mixture of terraced housing, 'villa' type semi-detached and a few detached. The heart of the area was Leicester Square or the 'Square' as it was referred to, and still is. Shops of all kinds could be found in the Square, hardware, greengrocer, post office, tobacconist, chemist, tea-room, tailor and an umbrella repair shop. Perhaps one of the Squares most notable features was the 'Green Man' or 'Pepper Pot' as it was nicknamed, an ornate circular cast iron Gents' urinal!

New Hampton Road West had clusters of small shops and came to be known as the 'West-Market'. Many of the smaller establishments had just a few shelves and a counter in someone's front room. The area even had its own cinema located in Coleman Street – The Strand as it was first known, later the West End, then the Park and finally the Rex.

The area's farming connection was frequently seen as herds of cattle and sheep were moved by drovers along streets and roads to the town's cattle market. Horden Road was the main route as it led to the farms and open countryside around Tettenhall and Claregate.

During the late nineteenth century employment could be found at the Woverhampton Steam Laundry in Sweetman Street or at Cookson's in Great Hampton Street. Large numbers of residents of Whitmore Reans and Dunstall worked on the railway at one of the two locomotive sheds at Stafford Road and Oxley. However, in 1924 The Courtaulds Company purchased the Dunstall Hall site and built a factory for the manufacturing of Rayon yarn. The area had been selected due to its high level of available female workers and in the years following the war employed a total of 2000, 500 of which were women. The factory chimneys were to become the unmistakable sign of the Whitmore Reans skyline up until when they were demolished in 1973 and the factory site became the Farndale housing estate.

Anthony Rose
July 2000

One
East to West
Through the Heart

Junction of Waterloo Road and New Hampton Road East, 1910. The large building in the distance is the Higher Grade School which was opened in 1894.

New Hampton Road East looking towards Waterloo Road, 1910. A builders's handcart can be seen 'parked' with freshly mixed cement and shovel in the gutter.

New Hampton Road East, c. 1921. The erection of pole supports for the overhead trolley system commenced in the borough on 26 January 1921 and the Whitmore Reans route was opened on the 28 August 1921. F. Campion, confectioners, can be seen on the corner of Dunkley Street while a tram car on route to town passes a Hansom Cab.

On the 20 May 1910 a large crowd gathered around the field directly opposite the Higher Grade School to witness the firing of the minute guns during the funeral of King Edward VII.

The Drill Hall, Devon Road, 1912. The Wolverhampton troop of the South Staffordshire Yeomanry preparing to ride off to camp on 19 May, photographed by their official photographer Mr Samuel Nightingale, who accompanied them on many occasions.

New Hampton Road at the junction with Kingsland Road and Leicester Street, 1925. In the far distance a tram makes its climb towards town while to the right of the picture a boy can be seen walking along the top of a wall. The building behind the boy is the Drill Hall and riding school.

Leicester Square, 1925. The gentleman on the bicycle is heading towards the park down Kingsland Road. The shop on the corner is the Home & Colonial Stores, one of many which could be found throughout the town. Next door is F.C. Reed, hairdresser; seventy-five years later the shop is still grooming the heads of the good folk of the area, but under new management.

All forms of transport of the day are captured in this view of the Square, 1912, including tram car No. 47 with its open vestibule and covered top deck, delivery cart, bicycle and pushchair. The horse drawn delivery van could well be from one of the numerous bakeries of the area, perhaps making a delivery to the Park Tea Rooms.

Park Tea Rooms, c. 1912. Located at the rear of the shops and accessed via the side entry, this must have been an ideal place to pause following a stroll around the park.

Leicester Square and Coleman Street, *c.* 1925. The most notable feature of the square was its circular cast iron gents' urinal that had numerous names. Two names that are printable are the 'Green Man' and the 'Pepper Pot' (From the collection of Wolverhampton Archives & Local Studies)

Coleman Street looking towards the junction with Chester Street in the 1960s. (From the collection of Wolverhampton Archives & Local Studies)

Modes perambulator shop, at the corner of New Hampton Road East and Walpole Street, *c.* 1920s. A public telephone box can be seen outside the Whitmore Reans Post Office. (From the collection of Wolverhampton Archives & Local Studies)

Leicester Square looking down New Hampton Road, 1965. A Sunbeam trolley bus No. 443 makes its way to Darlaston via Wolverhampton. In the background is the spire of Cranmer Methodist church.

Advertisement, c. 1900.

New Hampton Road looking towards Leicester Square, 1925. Two ladies pause in front of the grounds to St Andrew's vicarage.

New Hampton Road West, *c.* 1915. The tram-car No. 14 approaches the Hunter Street terminus. The Newbridge tram service had been cut back to Coleman Street in October 1903, but due to public pressure was extended on to Hunter Street in January 1905. There was an abundance of shops along New Hampton Road West, which resulted in the area being known as the 'West Market'.

Hunter Street junction with New Hampton Road, 1965. The junction marks the cross over from east to west

J. Ryans' grocery shop on the corner of Riches Street appears to be having a delivery of bread around 1915. The houses on the left were built around 1867, some of which are still standing today.

H. Ingram 'Fruiterer', 1925. Harry Ingram stands proudly outside his shop with his nephew Arthur who was born in Leeds in 1911. When Arthur's father died in France during the First World War, Arthur came to live in Whitmore Reans with his uncle.

Wesleyan Chapel around the 1900s, though it is better known today as Cranmer. The building to the left of the church is the Summer House public house which had a fine bowling green as did many of the public houses in the district.

WESLEYAN CHAPEL, NEWHAMPTON ROAD, WOLVERHAMPTON. 75

NEWBRIDGE(NEWHAMPTON ROAD CORNER) WOLVERHAMPTON.

End of the line, Tettenhall Road and in the distance its junction with New Hampton Road West, 1935.

Advertisement, c. 1900

Two
People and Events

Chester street cycling club, 1951. Those preparing to set off for a ride to Bridgnorth are: Peter Hughes, Pauline Martin, Alan Merrick, Irene Inscoe and Trevor Fullwood.

Brighton Villa, No. 215 New Hampton Road East, 1912. John Herbert Childs, aged four, poses for the photographer in front of the family home. The Child's family were salt merchants who ran the business from Railway Drive in the town.

It's a boy! John Herbert Childs, 1908.

John and his mother Mabel Louise Childs.
John's grandfather, John Childs, employed
Mabel in 1898 as housekeeper and
apparently told his son Isaac that you
should never let a good housekeeper go, so
Isaac married Mabel!

23

On the 7 June 1912 an addition to the family arrived, Joan Louise seen here with her brother and nanny in the garden of Brighton Villa.

The sitting room of No. 215 New Hampton Road West, 1965. Joan Childs, standing, is pictured with her mother Mabel and a friend.

Regularly seen and heard in Whitmore Reans during the 1930s was a lady known as 'Singing Margaret'. She had a very good voice in spite of her advanced age and would walk in the gutter dragging a box on a string behind her singing *'Tell me the old old story'*, and other such songs. Many residents helped her with food and clothes, which she preferred to money.

Typical of the housing of the area was the communal yard. On the left is the door to the brew house of No. 238 Waterloo Road, with a row of three water-closet doors. Pictured standing: Barbara Fullwood, Geoffrey Fullwood, seated: Mrs E.M. Minshall, Mrs E. Leason and Mr W. Leason.

Chester Street Coronation Party, June 1953, looking towards Gloucester Street.

The rear of No. 132 Lowe Street, 1930. Pictured is Ethel Stanley, her daughter Ethel (Cohen) and a local nurse.

Residents of Chester Street, June 1953, gather outside Baggott's off-licence to celebrate the Coronation. Note the Staffordshire blue brick pavement.

That's the way you do it! Rugby Street celebrates VE Day with a Punch and Judy show.

Samuel William Nightingale, photographer, pictured outside his glass 'Portrait Studio' in the garden of No. 45 Coleman Street. Today Samuel's grandson runs Nightingale Photographers from premises in Lower Street, Tettenhall.

The Drill Hall, Devon Road, 1 July 1911. The guard of honour present themselves for the official opening of the Drill Hall. In more modern times the building has been used as a telephone exchange, however today it lies empty with plans to redevelop the land for housing.

An interesting feature of this photograph is not so much the view but the caption at the bottom. The address given for Samuel Nightingale is No. 6 Bismarck Road – two years later the road was to be renamed on account of its German connection and is known today as Carter Road.

Following the opening ceremony a celebratory luncheon was held for the guests and Yeomanry.

Alderman Alan Davies seated at his desk at his home in Craddock Street. Alderman Davies worked for the Great Western Railway for fifty years starting as a messenger at Stafford Road in 1888. He became a member of Wolverhampton town council in 1919 and was elected mayor in 1929-1930.

The Davies family. From left to right, back row: Olive, Ivy, Nell, Flo, Nancy. Seated: Alderman Davies, Frank, Alan, Arthur, Mrs Eliza Davies.

Pictured outside their mothers' shop on the corner of Jackson Street and Lowe Street in 1925, are the Butler children, Eric, Phyllis and Vera.

Appley Cottage No. 134 Coleman Street, with Edith and Mabel Lumley around 1900.

The wedding group of Charles Lumley and Clara Garner pictured at the rear of the family warehouse in Coleman Street.

Coronation Sunday Parade, May 1953. A Brownie pack marching along New Hampton Road. Church Street parades were held almost every Sunday morning in the district, with everyone smartly attired in their uniforms.

Councillor Ted Mitchell receiving his chain of office, 22 May 1975.

Councillor Mitchell was one of a number of residents of the area who went on to become Mayor of Wolverhampton. In October 1975 the Mayor and Mayoress visited their old school, St Andrews, where the headmaster Mr Goodwin produced the 1925 school register.

Taylors Chemist shop at the corner of Hunter Street and New Hampton Road in the 1930s. Before the arrival of free health care the sick would seek the advice of their local chemists. Advice was free but recommended medicines had to be paid for. The most popular shop in the district was that run by Mr Lawley seen here outside his shop with his assistant Clifford Pope. Local people had great faith in him, in fact, one small girl appeared in his shop one day with a doll's pram in which lay the body of her dead kitten. She was sure that Mr Lawley would make it better!

Clifford Pope at the rear of Taylors Chemist, 1925.

The Stanley family in their garden at No. 385 New Hampton Road, 1937. The garden ran down to the rear of properties on Coleman Street. The building to the right behind the tree is that of St Andrews School, which in later years was taken over by the printers Barford and Newitt. On the far left is the rear of Whitmore Reans cinema.

Three
Out and About

Five Ways looking down Horden Road, 1963. The Five Ways public house is on the right and stood directly opposite the junction with Hunter Street. The Sunbeam trolley bus is on Route 7 Darlaston via Bilston. Trolley buses ceased on this route in August 1965.

Waterloo Road junction with Staveley Road in the 1920s. The house on the corner of Staveley Road has seen many changes; originally known as Kettering Villa, it later became the Redroofs Hotel and today is the Goal Post public house - a meeting place for a quick pint before going to the match.

Staveley Road, c. 1920. Staveley Road was originally known as Dunstall Lane and ran from North Street down past Dunstall Hall. With the exception of the first two houses on the left, the remaining houses still stand today. The entrance to Sherwood Street can be seen.

Bright Street, c. 1927. These houses were built around 1900. The majority of the housing in Whitmore Reans was small terrace-type buildings, erected as rented accommodation around 1880 with no inside sanitation. Sometimes there was a water tap in the backyard and shared outside toilet.

Leicester Street, 2 July 1914. The area around New Hampton Road was prone to flooding and this day was no exception. A freak storm in the middle of a heatwave had deluged the area. 'People ran helter-skelter, most of them being unprepared, wearing garments of the lightest material,' reported the *Express & Star*. For the children of the street it was an opportunity to have a cool paddle and pose for the photographer.

This map of 1919 shows how within seventy years the area had developed from that of the farmland of Whitmore End House to a street plan similar to that of today. ('Reproduced from

the 1919 Ordnance Survey map Crown Copyright')

Mrs Martin stands outside her house at No. 60 Chester Street in the 1930s. Streets of the district were named after large towns and cities, many other being named after local alderman and councillors of the day.

Clara Smith's shop in Evans Street, 1925. Throughout this book many views of Whitmore Reans can be found which have been taken from a fine series of photographs published by C. Smith. Quite fittingly this is No. 1 in the series, as the C. Smith is non other than Clara Smith who ran the second shop on the left, the corner shop being run by Mrs Whitehouse. Clara's was the kind of shop were you could find anything; old newspapers were piled high on the counter and store cupboards were crammed with all kinds of items, giving the impression that they would topple out once the cupboard door was opened.

St Winifred's girls home, c. 1919. The home was previously known as Whitmore Hall that had been built for Councillor Griffiths an ironmaster. The building had huge walls, which ran along Lowe Street with a drive up to the house via a gated entrance in Evans Street. The grounds were often used by local schools for nature trails and had a number of apple trees where much scrumping took place.

Lowe Street pictured from Dunstall Road, in the 1920s. The building on the left with the ornate lamp is the Junction Inn. A further three public houses were located in Lowe Street – The Grapes, Rose Tree, Yew Tree – as well as working men's club.

Phyllis Butler standing in the doorway of her mother's shop on the corner of Jackson Street and Lowe Street. The newspaper headlines help to date the picture to 1936; note the poster for the West End cinema.

Advertisement, c. 1900.

Courtaulds main entrance, Horden Road, 1927. Changes in women's fashions brought a huge demand for artificial 'silk' like materials such as rayon and nylon, and this demand coincided with the building of the Courtaulds factory on the site of the old Dunstall Hall.

Horden Road looking towards its junction with Court Road, 1963. The scene looks very different to that of today due to the lack of parked cars.

Sid Lumley's confectionery warehouse, Coleman Street in the 1930s. Joan and her sister Vera are taking time off from their duties in their father's warehouse to pose beside the new delivery van.

Devon Villa, No. 133A Coleman Street with a fine example of window furnishing. There is the drawn back lace blinds, upstairs and down, and the familiar pot plants on the windowsill.

Court Road in the spring of 1962. Trolly bus No. 477 is about to depart for Darlaston, via Bilston, on what was known as route 2. Two of Courtaulds chimneys dominate the skyline while a Co-op electric bakery delivery van is seen turning beyond a window cleaner's cart.

Court Road and its junction with New Hampton Road West, c. 1910. A family gathers to say their goodbyes, perhaps to relatives, who are leaving on a horse drawn cart.

Two views of Allen Road showing almost its complete length, *c.* 1912.

C. M. SHACKLOCK,

WOLVERHAMPTON & DISTRICT AGENT FOR

"LOCOMOBILE"
STEAM
CARRIAGES.

——

"MOORE
MOBILE,"
The New
CushionFrame
Bicycle.

——

"MILLENIUM,"
The
Wonderful
Puncture
Healer.

——

"FLEET" CYCLES
They hold
World's
Record
100 Miles
in
165 Minutes
at the
Crystal Palace
by
A. A. CHASE,
Nov. 9, 1901.

——

CANFIELD
FREE WHEEL
AND
BRAKE
COMBINED,
FITTED TO ANY
SAFETY FOR
20/-.

——

"STANDARD"
CYCLES
FROM £8.
Ladies' or Gents'
with
Free Wheel and
Two Brakes
£9.

——

GOLD MEDAL, GLASGOW EXHIBITION.
SILENT, ODOURLESS, CLIMB ANY HILL.

Price from £190 to £300.

Car always ready for trial run to intending Purchasers.

KLINGER GUAGES, CONDENSERS, BATTERIES, ACCUMULATORS.
REPAIRS, ACCESSORIES.   CYCLES FOR HIRE.
Carless Capel Petrol, and Pratt's Motor Spirit always in Stock.

"RUTLAND
REST"

——

H.M.S.
CYCLES
FROM
£10 10s.

——

INTERNATIONAL
MOTOR CARS.
The "Doctor's
Favorite."

——

MOTOR BICYCLES
FROM
£30 TO £50.

——

The "CHARETTE,"
(BRITISH MADE THROUGHOUT)

From 165 GUINEAS.

TRADESMEN'S 6-H.-P. DELIVERY VANS FROM 175 GUINEAS

TRIPS & TOURS ON MOTORS.   TERMS ON APPLICATION.

MANBY STREET WORKS, WOLVERHAMPTON.
3 Minutes' Walk from Exhibition Buildings.

Advertisement, c. 1900.

Coleman Street, 1967. Large-scale clearance of the district began in the mid-1960s. The new church of St Andrews was built in 1966 as the old church had been destroyed two years earlier by fire. The street lamp in the middle of the picture roughly marks where the West End cinema once stood, and the Round House public house is now the site of the service yard for the Avion Shopping centre.

The foundations for new housing on New Hampton Road opposite the Junction with Riches street, 1985.

Training Home for Orphan Girls, 1906. Situated in St Jude's Road the training home was built in 1879.

"THE HALF-WAY HOUSE"
TETTENHALL RD. WOLVERHAMPTON.   "BOWLING GREEN"

The Half Way House bowling green, 1911. The pub is situated halfway between London and Holyhead, hence the name. The houses in the background are those in Albert Road.

Four
Church and School

Until 1854 no religious services were held in Whitmore Reans, but in March of that year an afternoon service took place in a small room at No. 22 Coleman Street which was to continue for the next six years. The service was usually conducted by the curate-in-charge of St Peter's, however, in 1858 the Revd Julius Lloyd was appointed as curate-in-charge of the Whitmore Reans district, the population of which at that time was around 1,200. The Revd Lloyd continued the services in the Coleman Street house but accommodation was fast becoming insufficient. At a St Peter's parish meeting in March 1859 a committee was formed to take steps in building a church school at Whitmore Reans. Before the year was out land was purchased for £151 5s, and plans were prepared and an estimate to build was accepted from Messrs Higham for the sum of £598.

The church school opened for divine services on Sunday 1 July 1860, the preacher being the Ven. Archdeacon Moore, and the offertories were 'in aid of the purchase of a site for the erection of a church at Whitmore Reans at some future time'. On 24 May 1865, the foundation stone of the church of St Andrew, the Apostle, was laid and on St Andrew's Day, 30 November of that same year, Evening Prayers were held in the new church. It was not until the Revd W.H. Lowder took charge of St Andrew's district on 1 February 1866 that the daily service commenced.

Laying of the foundation stone of St Andrew the Apostle, Coleman Street, Wednesday 24 May 1865. The ceremony was performed by the Rector Revd J.H. Iles. For the previous five years, church services had been held in the school church which later became St Andrew's Infants Boys and Girls School which was situated in Coleman Street close to the junction with Evans and Gatis Street.

St Andrew's church and hall, 1911. The first vicar, Revd Bodington once described the church as 'a most unattractive building without a line of beauty about it.' In the background can be seen houses in Coleman Street. (Cheltenham Art Gallery & Museums Collection)

In 1874 the Revd Charles Bodington became involved in controversy over his use of ritualism in the services – he lit candles over the communion table, used unlawful vestments and read prayers with his back to the congregation, to name but a few. That year a Bill for the suppression of Ritualism had been passed under the Public Worship Regulation Act and some felt that the service at St Andrew's were too close to Roman Catholic practices. Charges were brought against the Revd Bodington and the case was heard in the Public Library at Lambeth Palace. Revd Bodington chose not to defend the case but instead held a well-attended service at St Andrew's where prayers were offered from seven o'clock in the morning until eight o'clock in the evening. The following week the case was quashed. The Revd Bodington wrote, 'the case was defended by the prayers of the faithful in St Andrew's Church.'

St Andrew's clergy, 1907. From left to right: Fr Ellies, Revd E.M. Baker, Fr Atkinson, -?-. Note the watch on the wrist of Fr Ellies. It was during the incumbency of the Revd Baker that the church opened the St Aidan's mission in Great Hampton Street.

Interior of St Andrew's, 1910.

The Lady Chapel, St Andrew's, 1910.
Following the church fire in 1964 the Lady
Chapel altar and two small stained glass
windows, one of St Andrew's, the other of St
Anne's as well as the original font were
relocated in the new church.

St Andrew's Churchmen's Club group with Revd Haden, 1904.

Numerous extensions to St Andrew's took place. This stone laying took place during the ministry of Fr Arthur James Longhurst, seen here on the far right during the 1920s.

St Andrew's church, Coleman Street, 1920. The caption to this postcard indicates that the building behind the women and children was St Andrew's Institute. In fact the building was known as the Armitage Hall which was built in 1904 as a gift from Dr Armitage of Waterloo Road.

A pram outside the vicarage door, 1912. The vicarage is the only part of the original church buildings that remains today, however it is subdivided into flats and no longer belongs to the church. (Cheltenham Art Gallery & Museums Collection)

Revd James V. Wilson and his wife Norah with their son Pat on the steps of St Andrew's vicarage, 1912. Revd Wilson was the brother of Dr Edward Wilson who died with Capt. Scott at the South Pole in 1912. Revd Wilson was much loved, not only by the congregation of St Andrew's, but also by the community of Whitmore Reans for the care he showed to the local men who went to fight in the First World War. (Cheltenham Art Gallery & Museums Collection)

St Andrew's Sunday School under a tree at Dunstall Hall with Fr Greening in 1915. (Cheltenham Art Gallery & Museums Collection)

The Revd Wilson wrote numerous letters back to his congregation during his time in France, many of which he specifically asked not to be published. However, in July 1916 he wrote: 'My Dear Friends, You will all be wondering what I have been doing during the past month, and how I have found everybody out here. As a matter of fact, I have found very few whom I knew before the War broke out. Most of our own St Andrew's men have either been killed or wounded in the battalion, and only their memory remains. There are a few left. I am sharing a billet now with the Adjutant of the 1/6 S. Staffs., Captain Piper, and all old St Andrew's boys will like to know that he is fit and well and as active and keen as ever on his job. St Andrew's may well be proud of having so smart an officer out here. Sergeant Merrick is in C Company, and it is a real joy to find a Churchman of his type using his influence in the battalion. There are a good many of our old schoolboys here as well, and I am gradually finding them out. The sad thing is to know of the gaps in the ranks of the battalion, gaps so recently made and many which again bring sorrow to our Whitmore Reans homes'.

St Andrew's church, Coleman Street, Sunday 31 May 1964. Fire devastated the whole of the east-end of the church, destroying beyond repair the Kempe Window, organ, choir screen and magnificent rood.

The decision to build a new church was unanimous, and in 1966 the ruins of the old church were finally demolished. During the demolition a jar was found behind the consecration stone, which contained a hand written list of St Andrew's congregation and a service paper of the final dedication and consecration of the chancel in 1890, along with other mementoes of the occasion. The jar was put back behind the original stone, which was built into the east wall of the new church.

St Andrew's Church Lads Brigade with the Revd James Wilson in full army uniform, 1914. St Andrew's CLB was formed in 1900 under Lt Crombie and Col.-Sgt King; in those early years the movement was closely identified with the Army, particularly with the Cadet Force. In November 1901 the vicar Fr Haden wrote in the church magazine: 'Church Lads Brigade. At last we are contented: in fact we are happy, for we have attained the height of ambition. The War Office listened to the importunate demand of the Vicar, and have sent us a case of beautiful carbines... no-one can smile at us as only imitation soldiers, and we shall be proud to march out with real guns all our own, even though they be a considerable weight to carry'.

Company Staff, 1959. From left to right, back row: Drum Major Frank Clarke, Sgt Roy Blower, Band Sgt Stan Clarke, Sgt Ken Lawley. Front row: Lt Ken Crane, Revd Hugh Bower, Capt. Tony Crane

St Andrew's CLB full company, 1959. The company was made up of three groups: the group for the youngest members, 8-11 year olds was called the Young Boys Corps, their uniform consisted of a cap and belt. The group for 11-14 year olds Junior Training Corps wore side cap and uniform. Then for the oldest members, 14 year olds and above, there was the CLB Uniform with peaked cap.

CLB camp Towyn near Ryhl, 1949.

Early morning PT at Towyn, 1949.

Weston-Super-Mare camp, 1952.

Sunday morning parade corner of Dunstall Road and Gloucester Street, 1966. The weekly parade through the streets was always certain to produce a group of followers.

St Andrew's annual Singles v Married men's football match, 1953. The match took place on the Railway Football pitch at the bottom of Horden Road. This is probably the singles team as the lads are smiling. Tony Crane pictured here on the back row far right was transferred two years later!

The Battalion cross-country team, 1953. From left to right, back row: Tony Crane, Revd David Smith, Stan Clarke, H. Williams (company commander).

St Andrew's summer fete, 1952. Pictured here is the committee responsible for selecting the 'Rose Queen' – Revd David Smith, Miss Bibb, Mr Sanders and Mrs Smith. The two gentlemen on the left are Fred Sexton and Harry Thorley.

And this year's Rose Queen is…

Kathleen Law 'Rose Queen' for 1952.

The Rose Queen group with Margaret Mantle forth from the right and her sister Wendy second from the right.

The Church Lads Brigade prepares to parade along New Hampton Road toward Leicester Square.

The newly crowned Queen, Kathleen Law, with her maids in waiting, begin their 'walk about' of the district.

St Andrew's Church Infants Sunday School Parade, Leicester Street. The pipe smoking gentleman in the middle of the picture is Harry Cohen.

St Andrew's CLB, lead by Band Sgt Stan Clarke in the 'Pear Drop' Gatis Street, July 1953.

St Andrew's School dance team. This happy group of girls danced on the 'hallowed' turf of the Molineux football ground in 1937 to celebrate the Coronation of George VI.

The dance team during rehearsals on the lawn of St Andrew's church.

St Andrew's barge trip weekend aboard the *Ernest Thomas* from Aldersley to Wheaton Aston in 1955.

The hot summer of 1955 meant that the canal had low water, which resulted in the barge not being able to turn around at its usual point. This meant a very late arrival back at Aldersley on Sunday evening and the above boys were greeted by a group of anxious parents.

Four 'willing' volunteers set about pealing the spuds, they didn't mind as long as their mothers didn't find out!

Final count, will there be enough?

St Andrew's drama club, 1951. Amongst those present are Mrs Smith, June Davies, Jennifer Weaver, Hilda Cohen, Margaret Turner, Mr Sanders, Harry Thorley, Fred Rodgers and Mr Lampitt.

A scene from a two-act play entitled *The Right Stuff* put on in the Armitage Hall of St Andrew's church in February 1952.

St Andrew's Choir, *c*. 1900.

St Andrew's choir in the 1960s. From left to right, back row: Michael Hall, Charlie Butler, Arnold Collett, June Garbitt, Bill Rose, Geoffrey Butler, and organist Bill Duncombe. Amongst the others present are Elaine Wainwright, Ruth Lewis, Lynn Wainwright, and Revd Hugh Bower.

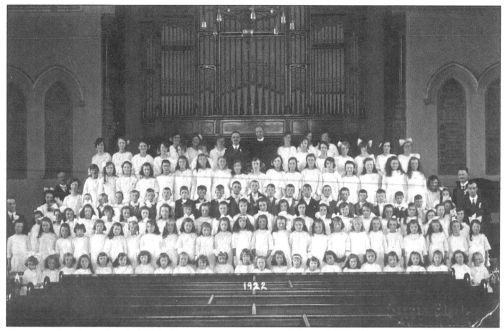

Cranmer Sunday school, 1922. Cranmer was renowned throughout the area for its large Sunday school attendance.

Wesleyan Chapel, New Hampton Road West.

Members of the Tabernacle Baptist church, Dunstall Road, c. 1910. The Tabernacle church was founded in June 1908 when forty worshippers met in the Molineux Hall, Molineux Street, and decided to form a church. In 1909 the Church purchased land on the corner of Dunstall Road with a view to the building of a church.

The Tabernacle Band of Hope, Dunstall Road in 1914. In 1911 the Unitarian church in Bath Road became vacant and the Baptist church committee decided to purchase the building and have it re-erected on its own site in Dunstall Road.

Revd Sidney Charles Cook with a fine 'Tab' harvest in the 1920s.

The first full-time Pastor, Revd S.C. Cook officiated at the stone laying of the new Tabernacle church, Dunstall Road on 12 September 1931.

Dunstall Road Boys Brigade was formed in 1927 and is seen here on the steps of the church in 1948. Great rivalry existed in the district between Church groups, none more so than between the Church Lad's Brigade of St Andrew's and the Boys' Brigade of the Tabernacle. From left to right, front row: Leo Gregson, Len Cartwright, Bert Ball, Revd Garfield Evans, George Turvey, Horace Simkin.

Baptist Tabernacle Sunday school anniversary in 1945 pictured outside the house on the corner of Leicester Street and Dunstall Road.

The 5th Wolverhampton Company of the Girls' Life Brigade Cadets in 1951, pictured on the steps of the Baptist church, Dunstall Road.

Girls' Life Brigade, 1951. The Brigade was formed at the same time as the Boys Brigade in 1927.

Christ Church, Five Ways, c. 1930. The church was built in 1867 and stood on the corner of Dunstall Road and Waterloo Road. It was classed as High Church similar to St Andrew's, and like the Revd Bodington at that church, the Revd Glover of Christ Church came into conflict with some of his congregation for Ritualism during the service.

The High Altar of Christ Church, 1907.

The Wolverhampton 16th Scout Troop pictured in the playground of Christ Church Junior School in Leicester Street, 1934. Pictured in the back row from the flag on the left: S. Southwell, F. Townsend, W. Durnall, W. Lovell, W. Walton, -?-, J. Holland. Seated behind the big drum is Anker Nixon who was the scoutmaster and Christ Church verger.

The 16th Wolverhampton Scout Troop Cub Pack, Christ Church School, 1937. From left to right, back row: K. Marshall, L. Painter, R. Southwell, F. Westwood, T. Easson, B. Churchman, -?-, K. Westwood. Middle row: T. Bruen, B. Tomkys, -?-, -?-, -?-, J. Slater, G. Mayes, J. David. Front row: A. Churchman, M. Goodman, V. Goodman, Revd C. Lacey, W. Lovell, G. Fullwood.

Interior of Christ Church, c. 1930. The church was demolished in 1975 and a mosque now stands on the site.

Christ Church Infants School Group 2, Leicester Street, *c.* 1905. The little chap sixth from the left on the back row, is Berty Ball who was born in 1899.

Christ Church School. 1949. From left to right, back row: Iris Lees, Brenda Townsend, Pat Snape, Elsie Muir, Janet Downes, Kathleen Ward, Thelma Hood, Hazel Winfield, Kathleen Lucas, Pauline Martin, Pat Davies, Ann Dolan, Ilene Turner. Middle row: Jonathan Bradbury, John Stevens, Tony Palmer, Irene Chitty, Brenda Jones, Christine Smith, Helen Clapp, Anne Rowley, Arthur Rudkin, David Jarrett, Walter Jones, Michael Clarke, George Newman. Front row: Alan Wood, Michael Cooper, John Lucas, Tony Deans, John Matthews, Peter Lowbridge, Gordon Cooper, Godfrey Hult, Robert Nixon, Walter Lane, Graham Ling, Robert Cope, Edward Taylor.

St Andrew's Girls, Gatis Street, 1920s.

Another school group taken in the 1920s in the playground of St Andrew's, Gatis Street.

St Andrew's School, Coleman Street, 1926. The boy smiling on the front row far left is Ted Mitchell who became town mayor in 1975.

A classroom in St Andrew's, Gatis Street, 1927. Ethel Stanley is fifth from the left, seen standing with a badge on her pinafore. In her working life Ethel became school secretary, and

St Andrew's, Gatis Street, 1933. On the far left is Mr Bennett the class teacher and on the far right is Frank Wilson, headteacher. The school is now known as Farndale.

with her husband Harry Cohen, they were long serving members of the congregation of St Andrew's church.

St Andrew's School carnival float prior to moving off to join the Church Carnival street parade.

Vikings pose for a photograph, before setting off on a 'pillaging' trip around the streets of Whitmore Reans, all under the watchful of eye of Mrs Ethel Cohen the school secretary.

John Lewis seen clowning around, 1964.

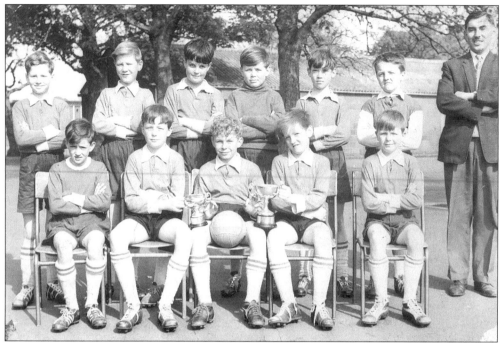

St Andrew's School football team, 1965. The team achieved the double winning of both the league and the Blakemore Cup. From left to right, back row: R. Key, P. Guard, N. Bower, M. Link, B. Mcallen, M. Reynolds, Mr Lewis. Front row: G. Page, B. Hughes, R. Page, S. Roffey, A. Hughes.

St Andrew's football team leaving Dunstall Race Course after winning the Cup, 1965.

Classroom of Horden Road School, 1925. The girl standing by the window is Joan Lumley. The school later became known as Whitmore and is now St Andrew's.

St Jude's School. The children appear to be dressed in their best for the occasion, and the number of sailor suits suggest this to be a Victorian photograph.

St Andrew's School, 1966.

St Andrew's staff in the 1970s. From left to right, back row: -?-, Mary Webb, Peter Thrussel, Lynda White, Ethel Butler, -?-. Middle row: Mrs Wall, Mary Lewis, Mr David, John Hawkins, John Smith, June Garbitt, -?-, Mrs Heath. Front row: -?-, Sheila Bragger, Ann Seniuta, Albert Goodwin, Mrs Jones, Ann Cunlith, Claud Ford.

Five
The Park

The West Park was opened to the public on Whit Monday, 6 June 1881, and from that day to the present the park has always been regarded as a special place to the residents of Whitmore Reans. Its flowerbeds and lawns have always been immaculately kept. Many people of the district enjoyed walking, with Horden Road, Gorsebrook Road, Tettenhall Road and New Hampton Road being the most popular route. Each Sunday evening a brass band played in the bandstand becoming a very popular attraction.

Conservatory, West Park, Wolverhampton.

The fine Victorian conservatory in 1928. The conservatory was built from the proceeds of the 1893 Floral Fete at a cost of £1,500. Mrs Dickinson, the widow of Alderman Samuel Dickinson who played a major role in acquiring the park for the town, officially opened it in July 1896.

The park lake and island, 1952. Due to the original swampy nature of the area, the forming of a lake was not a difficult task. The supply of water into the lake was increased by way of water from a well at the nearby public baths.

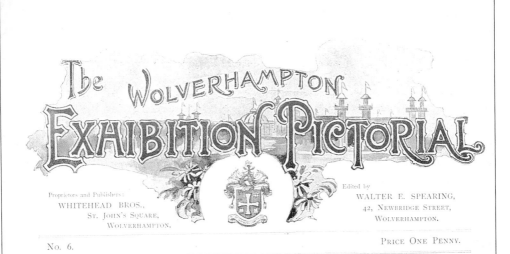

The WOLVERHAMPTON EXHIBITION PICTORIAL

Proprietors and Publishers:
WHITEHEAD BROS.,
St. John's Square,
Wolverhampton.

Edited by
WALTER E. SPEARING,
42, Newbridge Street,
Wolverhampton.

No. 6.

Price One Penny.

The Kiosk Bandstand.

Photo. by

Whitlock, Wolverhampton.

The 'Wolverhampton Exhibition Pictorial' produced to accompany the Art & Industrial Exhibition of 1902.

The Wolverhampton Art & Industrial Exhibition, 1902. Opened in May the exhibition was designed to show off the town's industrial output. Previous exhibitions in the town had been very successful and profitable and therefore there were no shortage of backers. Unfortunately the backers had not allowed for the weather and due to one of the worst summers on record the exhibition was a financial disaster losing the then enormous sum of £30,000.

Building of the Industrial Hall, February 1902.

The Duke of Connaught, King Edward VII's brother, opened the exhibition with a solid gold key. Such was the anticipation of large crowds attending the exhibition that a new section of tramway was opened on the same day as the exhibition, and ran from Victoria Square to Coleman Street via New Hampton Road East.

The arrival of the Duke and Duchess at the Concert Hall. In the background can be seen Waterloo Terrace which stands on New Hampton Road and was built around 1855.

The exhibition was the biggest to be staged in the country since the Great Exhibition of 1851. The Industrial Halls featured trade and industry from all over the Midlands area. There was also International Pavilions from Russia, Canada and Japan.

The Canadian Pavilion.

The exhibition had numerous attractions, one of the most popular being the Canadian water chute. Boats were winched up the chute and then released to slide down at speed into the lake. Unfortunately there was one sad occurrence, a boat carrying Col. Thorneycroft of Tettenhall Towers entered the water almost side-on, throwing the Colonel against the side of the boat. He received a blow to the head and never properly recovered and died on 6 February 1903.

Another popular attraction was a maze which had the title of the 'House of Many troubles'

During the evenings over 20,000 electric coloured lamps illuminated the buildings and grounds.

On Saturday 9 August 1902, thousands of people attended the exhibition to celebrate the Coronation of Edward VII. The grounds were open from ten o'clock in the morning, until eleven in the evening and visitors were entertained by a huge firework display.

There was a feast of daily entertainment; one such item was a Brass Band Contest which according to the 'Exhibition Pictorial' was 'something novel for Wolverhampton' Pictured here is the 'Romanian Orchestra'

Centre Beds, West Park, Wolverhampton.

PUBLISHED BY C. SMITH

The unmistakable feature of the Park Clock and flower beds in the 1920s.

Pictured here at the park, is the arrival a large floral crown, which was to be the centrepiece of the flowerbeds celebrating the Coronation of King George V in 1911.

THE BRIDGE, WEST PARK, WOLVERHAMPTON.

Dark days were on the horizon when this picture was taken in 1914, with the coming of the First World War. However, all seems tranquil in the park.

Six
Work

Horden Road, main entrance to Courtaulds in the 1960s. After the First World War the demand for rayon increased and the Courtaulds Company built new factories, the largest being built on the site of the old Dunstall Hall. Building began in 1924 and the first viscose rayon yarn was produced there in 1926. During the Second World War large areas of the factory were requisitioned for the Admiralty and other services.

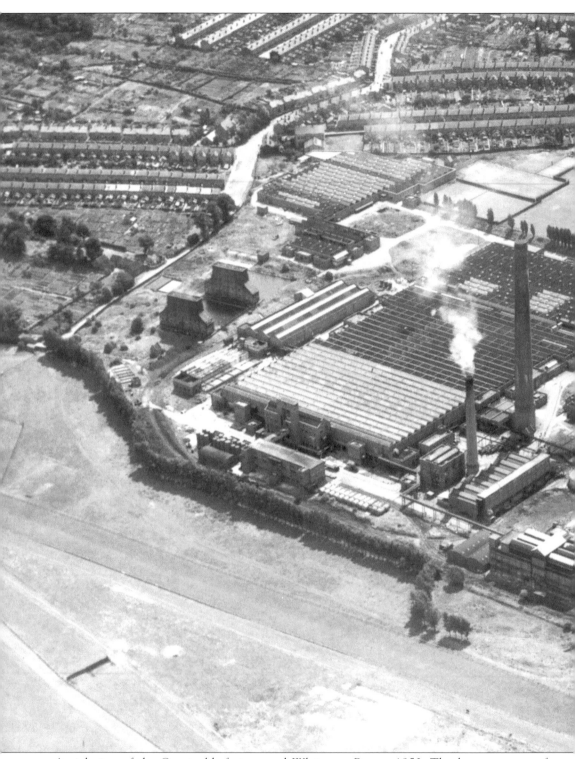

Aerial view of the Courtaulds factory and Whitmore Reans, 1950. The large expanse of land in the centre of the picture is the factories sports ground. There are very few of the

old landmarks of the district left.

A familiar sight to so many as they past through the main gates in the 1950s. The chimneys were known as the 'Three Sisters' and were demolished on 17 June 1973.

The Yarn Reeling room, 1930.

Coronation Day, 1952.

The Three Sisters in the 1960s. The grandstand of the racecourse can be seen on the left with St Peter's church in the distance on the right.

Courtaulds football team, 1927-1928.

Courtaulds long service employees at Wolverhampton Railway Station before leaving for the award ceremony which was held in London in 1967. Those present are Miss D.V. Roberts, Miss E.M. Taylor, Mr W. New, Mr D. Ward, Mr R.W. Wiggin, Mr W. Lewis, Mr D. Mallen, Mr M.R. Pritchard, Mr R.J. Adams, Mr W.H. Reynolds, Mr H. Lander, Mr D.H. Currell, Mr H. Hales, Mr W.R. Collier, Mr G. Knight, Mr J. Smith, Mr E.C. Askey.

Just beyond the main gate and in front of the office block, 1950. This area is now the entrance to the Farndale Housing Estate and the site of Firsbrook House.

The frilled curtains and collar finishing room, Wolverhampton Steam Laundry, 1902.

The wash house, Wolverhampton steam Laundry, Sweetman Street, 1902.

Seven

Dunstall

The area of Dunstall or Tunstall, as it was originally known, is closely linked to the history of Wolverhampton and in particular that of Lady Wulfruna. A theory is that she may have lived there, looking out across 'Wulfrun's meadow' to the hill a mile away, which was soon to be crowned with her church. There were many stories connecting Lady Wulfruna with Dunstall Hall, one of which was that an underground passage existed connecting the hall with St Peter's church which she would use in bad weather.

In his 1836 account of the Collegiate church, Dr Oliver refers to the beautiful spring at Dunstall, which was once the favourite resort of Lady Wulfruna. Due to its connection with her the spring acquired the reputation of possessing miraculous virtues. In 1901 Sir Alexander Staveley Hill erected a stone head in Gorsebrook Road, Wulfruna's Well, at what was supposed to be the source of the River Smestall better known as the Smestow Brook. But if anything, the area of Dunstall was better known as being the home of Wolverhampton's racecourse since 1886.

The Lake at Dunstall Hall, 1915.

Dunstall Hall, 1914. There had been a house on this site since the time of Henry II when it was in the hands of a family who took their name from the town of Hampton. In 1640 the house came into the possession of the Wightwick family who in 1813 sold it to the banker, Henry Horden. Very little of the original house remained and it was Horden who built this fine moated Hall in 1826. The Hall was demolished around 1915 and the Courtualds factory built on the site. (From the collection of Wolverhampton Archives & Local Studies)

Dunstall Road, 1913. The large house in the background is 'Rosedale', which George Luce had built for his family in 1910, paying the builders in golden guineas as it was built. George Luce was the proprietor of Luce's Bakery in Craddock Street, which caught fire in 1937. The Luce family moved from 'Rosedale' in the 1920s, selling the house to Mr and Mrs Charles Hayward, who later had a son, Jack.

George Luce was Mayor from 1939-1942 and is seen here with the King and Queen at Molineux on the occasion of the Wolves winning the War League Cup in 1942 after playing Sunderland in front of seventy-five thousand spectators.

Jack Thomas outside his shop on the corner of Craddock Street in 1959. During the 1920s the shop was better known as Speak's Dairy.

Dunstall Players, 1949. This local group of thespians were always well received in the area and put on three productions a year. From left to right, back row: B. Massey, P. Watkins, G. Fullwood, R. Nokes. Middle row: E. Whitehouse, M. Watkins, A. Watkins and Betty, W. Massey, E. Allen, D. Potts, W. Minshall, G. Powis, A. Chambers, E. Stokes. Front row seated: E. Farrell, L. Hawkswood, B. Fullwood, J. Harper, J. Nixon, A. Richards, E. Whitehouse, C. Richards, D. Hands, E. Stokes. On floor: R. Price, E. Nokes, J. Hardwick.

"GRAND NATIONAL NIGHT"
By DOROTHY & CAMPBELL CHRISTIE

CHARACTERS
(In the order of their appearance)

Morton	EDWIN WHITEHOUSE
Gerald Coates	PETER WATKINS
Babs Coates	DOROTHY HAND
Philip Balfour	DAVID POTTS
Joyce Penrose	JOAN HARPER
Buns Darling	BRYAN MASSEY
Pinkie Collins	EDNA STOKES
Detective Inspector Ayling	GEORGE POWIS
Sergeant Gibson	EDGAR ALLEN

Produced by MOLLIE WATKINS.

China and Glassware kindly loaned by
C. J. BEAVIS LTD., LICHFIELD STREET, WOLVERHAMPTON.

Furniture kindly loaned by
DEVITT'S FURNISHERS, 35, PENN ROAD, WOLVERHAMPTON.

SYNOPSIS OF SCENES

*The action of the play passes in the study of Gerald
Coates' house in Chillington, near Liverpool.*

PROLOGUE.—The night of Friday, March 27th.

ACT I   Scene 1. The evening of Saturday, March 28th.
       Scene 2. The same evening (two and a half hours later).

ACT II   The morning of Monday, April 6th.

ACT III   The same day (early afternoon).

Scenery designed and executed by our
STAGE STAFF.

Amplification System supplied by
NOKES RADIO AND ELECTRICAL SERVICE
163, STAFFORD ROAD, BUSHBURY.   Phone 23396

Programme for the 1948 Dunstall Players production of 'Grand National Night'.

Wulfruna's Well, Gorsebrook Road. Over the years there has been many requests to move this monument to a more 'suitable' site. However, what's more suitable than the site it was intended for?

The local 'bobby' Reg Chetter of Gorsebrook Road seated at the wheel of Wolverhampton's first police car.

Carter Road, 1914. This road today, apart from the inevitable rough casting of walls and the disappearance of front wall railings, is unchanged to those days when it was original known as Bismarck Road.

Carter Road VE party celebrations. The three ladies, from left to right: Mrs Jones, Mrs Sullivan, Mrs Timmins.

Oxley Manor was built in 1854 and stood on what is now Oxley golf course. Sir Alexander Staveley Hill, first Chairman of the Wolverhampton Racecourse Company, moved there after selling the Dunstall Park Estate for £36,000 to the newly formed Wolverhampton Racecourse and Dunstall Park Club Limited. The house was demolished in 1929.

Sir Alexander Staveley Hill, who was born at Dunstall Hall in 1825.

Main Entrance, Dunstall Park, Wolverhampton.

10.   PUBLISHED BY C. SMIT.

The Lodge and main entrance to Dunstall Park racecourse, 1913. Since redevelopment of the racecourse the lodge is the only remaining feature of this postcard view from the Clara Smith series. However, the gates have been relocated and are the entrance to the new all-weather racecourse.

INSPECTING THE FLYING MACHINES AT DUNSTALL PARK.

Dunstall Park, first Midland aviation meeting, June 1910. A number of large hangers were erected on the racecourse for one of the country's first aviation meetings. The event drew large crowds for the flying week, defying the atrocious weather conditions.

118

Many popular aviators of the day attended the meeting, including the Hon. Charles Rolls who earlier that same month had achieved the first double channel crossing. Unfortunately two weeks after taking part at Dunstall he was killed at a similar event in Bournemouth.

Flying at Dunstall Park, Wolverhampton, Aviation Meeting June, 1910.

Prize money totalling £3,000 drew a range of flying machines, the largest prize going to the aviator who remained airborne for the longest time in total during the week. This was won by Grahame White flying a Farman.

119

Over the years there has been a number of attempts to close Dunstall Park racecourse and develop the land. None was stronger than the attempt made by the millionaires, the Richardson twins in 1987 to turn the 130 acres into a retail park. Such was local feeling against the plans that the 'Dunstall Park Action Group' was formed to fight any such development. With the support of residents, local councillors and MPs, council planners finally rejected the scheme. The course was eventually taken over by the Ram Racecourse company who redeveloped the site into Europe's first all-weather floodlit track with a large proportion of the land being developed for housing. Her Majesty the Queen officially opened the new course in June 1994.

Dunstall Park pigeon lofts, *c.* 1928.
Pigeon racing was a very popular sport in
and around the Wolverhampton area
and none so more than in the Dunstall
Hill area known as the 'Garden Hills'.
Here a proud owner displays his trophies
and champion birds.

Dunstall racecourse club building in the 1980s. The racecourse was the venue for many events
including vintage car rallies and dog shows. This area is now a housing estate.

The racecourse as seen from Gorsebrook Road, 1985. The grandstands were built by Henry Willcock a local builder in 1888, but were all demolished to make way for yet another housing estate.

Oxley viaduct, 1965. Below are the backs of houses in Jones Road while an engine makes its way across towards the Stafford Road sheds.

During the 1920s Broncho Bill's Circus made their home in Wolverhampton and had a yard in Gorsebrook Road adjacent to the railway viaduct where the animals were 'wintered'. Two stars of the circus were 'Salt and Saucy' who became well known to residents due to their regular walks around the district. Jones Road can be seen in the background.

Saucy puts one past the keeper, with the horse box entrance to the racecourse and the railway viaduct in the background.

John Swallow alias 'Broncho Bill' who came to live in Waterloo Road in the 1920s and whose grandson still lives in the town.

Broncho Bill sitting amongst his Wild West Show team, some of whom had lodgings in Whitmore Reans during the winter months.

Animals were housed inside the tin shed accommodation in Gorsebrook Road, which today is a motor repair garage.

A circus artist during winter training.

The entrance to the G.W.R. Institute, 20 January 1932. The Institute was erected on the site of the former toll-house on the Stafford Road. The low bridge seen to the right was replaced by a higher structure the following year to allow double-decker trolley buses to pass.

Stafford Road at its junction with Gorsebrook Road in the 1930s. The Bridge Inn is on the right directly opposite Gorsebrook Road.

Aerial view of Whitmore Reans and Dunstall, 1992. The two high-rise flats stand roughly where Whitmore End House stood almost 160 years ago.

Acknowledgements

In 1995 I helped to organize an exhibition entitled 'Whitmore Reans Then and Now' which was held at St Andrew's church during the districts City Challenge Unity Weekend. Since that event I have been approached on numerous occasions to consider compiling a book – well here it is.

I have had enormous pleasure in collecting the material presented here, which has also allowed me to meet with such a delightful number of people, to you all I offer my thanks and best wishes. Special thanks to Mr Harry Blewitt for access to his marvellous postcard collection and that of Eric Woolley.

Thanks also to, Miss M. Taylor, Mrs W. Tomling, Mrs M. Timmins, Mr M. Butler, Bill Duncombe, Miss J. Childs, John Swallow, Mr and Mrs Mitchell, Pat Davies, Simon Dewey, Mr Nightingale, Mrs P. Smith, Mr and Mrs R. Lewis, Margery Pickering, Mrs Pope, Mrs J. Evans, Tony Crane, Mr M. Sedgemore, Mrs N. Crane, Mrs D. Harvey, Mrs H. Cheese, Mrs Thomson, Mrs E. Neach, Mr and Mrs G. Fullwood, Mr B. Jones, Ken Chetter, Keith Hoult, Mrs Tate, Mrs Tonks, Mrs D. Evans, Joan Smith, Mrs A. Barnett, Mrs M. Wallet, Lynn Vaughan, Mrs Goodwin, Albert Robins, Mervyn Strodzinsky, Janet Gasper, Mrs Howell, Express & Star, DPAG, Courtaulds Photographic Library, The Wilson Collection, and not forgetting the congregation of St. Andrew's church.

I sincerely hope that I have not missed anyone out, but if I have, I apologise.